SUPER CHEF

The Cooking of
GREECE

This book is dedicated to my sister Joanne.

This author's sincere gratitude to Peter Mavrikis, Michelle Bisson, Kay Petronio, and Anahid Hamparian.

Published by Marshall Cavendish Benchmark
An imprint of Marshall Cavendish Corporation
All rights reserved.

Website: www.marshallcavendish.us

Text © 2012 by Matthew Locricchio

Food photographs © 2012 Jack McConnell, McConnell, McNamara & Company
Map © 2012 by Mike Reagan
Illustrations by Janet Hamlin
Illustrations © 2012 by Marshall Cavendish Corporation

This publication represents the opinions and views of the author based on Matthew Locricchio's personal experience, knowledge, and research. The information in this book serves as a general guide only. The author and publisher have used their best efforts in preparing this book and disclaim liability rising directly and indirectly from the use and application of this book.

Other Marshall Cavendish Offices:
Marshall Cavendish International (Asia) Private Limited, 1 New Industrial Road, Singapore 536196 • Marshall Cavendish International (Thailand) Co Ltd. 253 Asoke, 12th Flr, Sukhumvit 21 Road, Klongtoey Nua, Wattana, Bangkok 10110, Thailand • Marshall Cavendish (Malaysia) Sdn Bhd, Times Subang, Lot 46, Subang Hi-Tech Industrial Park, Batu Tiga, 40000 Shah Alam, Selangor Darul Ehsan, Malaysia

Marshall Cavendish is a trademark of Times Publishing Limited
All websites were available and accurate when this book was sent to press.

Library of Congress Cataloging-in-Publication Data

Locricchio, Matthew.
   The cooking of Greece / Matthew Locricchio.
     p. cm. — (Superchef—2nd ed.)
   Summary: "Introduces the different culinary regions of Greece and presents many kinds of recipes for traditional Greek dishes"— Provided by publisher.
   Includes bibliographical references and index.
   ISBN 978-1-60870-552-8 (print) — ISBN 978-1-60870-740-9 (ebook) 1. Cooking, Greek—Juvenile literature. 2. Cooking, Mediterranean—Juvenile literature. 3. Food habits—Greece—Juvenile literature. I. Title.
   TX723.5.G8L63 2012
   641.59495—dc22
          2010052548

Editor: Peter Mavrikis
Publisher: Michelle Bisson
Art Director: Anahid Hamparian
Series design by Kay Petronio
Art direction for food photography by Matthew Locricchio
Food styling by Marie Hirschfeld and Matthew Locricchio

Photo Credits: Nikos Pavlakis/Alamy: 14; Greece/Alamy: 17; Mayday/Alamy: 19; Matthew Locricchio: 76; Photka/Fotolia: 90, 91, 92; Elena Schweitzer/Fotolia: 91; Dmitriy Kosterev/Fotolia: 92; Peter Jameson: 96.

Printed in Malaysia (T)
135642

SUPER CHEF

The Cooking of
GREECE

second edition
Matthew Locricchio

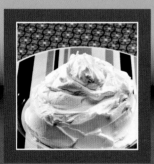

with photos by Jack McConnell

Marshall Cavendish
Benchmark

New York

Contents

Dear Reader,

I can't think of a better way to learn about a culture first-hand than to cook and savor its cuisine. Understanding the breadth of Italian pasta varieties, or Greek phyllo specialties and greens dishes, of Chinese dumplings, Indian curries, Thai spice blends, and more helps us understand something about the geography, history, and soul of a country.

My first memories of food come from my own family, of Sunday meals that lasted half the day and holidays that required a week of cooking. There was a rhythm to the dishes we ate depending on the time of year, with specific sweets for Christmas, breads for New Year's, and the vegan fare my grandmother would prepare as we fasted for Easter. For me, food became synonymous with both communicating and sharing. The dinner table was a time of talking about the issues of the day. The holidays and impromptu visits by family and friends became reason to put a little something on the table for others to enjoy. Those are important lessons to carry through life and they are learned young. As a kid I always helped in the kitchen, regardless of whether I wanted to or not! Thanks to that I learned to cook fairly young, and by the time I was a teenager, I was inviting my friends over to try my own creations.

Young people today are much more food savvy than I was way back in the 1960s and 1970s. Teenagers have a much broader experience with ethnic foods than I ever did. There was no such thing as organic food when I was growing up. We also did not have access to the constant stream of information available today. Ironically, with the overabundance of information out there on food, there is very little real knowledge about how to cook simple, healthy, good food.

The Superchef series of cookbooks aims to do just that and in the process show young people that the world is, indeed, one delicious kitchen where many different cooking traditions flourish.

Cooking is an art, but it's also more than that. People can live without music, paintings, sculpture, and literature, but we can't live without food! So, enjoy the process, but better yet, enjoy sharing it with others.

Diane Kochilas

Consulting chef
Pylos Restaurant, NYC

Diane Kochilas is a chef, author, and teacher. She has published over a dozen cookbooks including, *The Food and Wine of Greece*, *The Greek Vegetarian*, *Meze*, *The Glorious Foods of Greece*, *Mediterranean Grilling* and more. Diane has also made numerous television and radio appearances, and runs a cooking school focusing on traditional Greek recipes, as well as the culture of Greece. To learn more about Diane, go to www.dianekochilas.com.

SUPER
CHEF

Welcome to the second edition of Superchef. When we first created this series of cookbooks our goal was to introduce new cooks to traditional yet tantalizing recipes from around the world, adapted to work in your kitchen. That goal has not changed.

Young chefs like yourself who discovered Superchef have been learning to cook international recipes with family and friends ever since. The world of satisfying recipes, along with the basic principles of kitchen safety, food handling, and common-sense nutrition is what made Superchef so popular when it was first introduced. Those same goals hold true with the new edition.

Learning to master authentic international recipes and sharing them with family and friends is the motivation behind these cookbooks. This edition offers the invitation to new cooks as well as old to step into the kitchen and start cooking. Within this complete series you will find classic recipes from eight different countries. The recipes are not necessarily all low-fat or low-calorie, but they are all healthful. Even if you are a vegetarian, you will find recipes without meat or with suggestions to make the dish meatless.

Superchef can change the way you feel about cooking. You can learn to make authentic and delicious dishes from recipes that have been tested by young cooks in kitchens like yours. The recipes range from very basic to challenging. The instructions take you through the preparation of each dish step by step. Once you learn the basic techniques of the recipes, you will understand the principles of cooking fresh food successfully.

There is no better way to get to know people than to share a meal with them. Today, more than ever, it is essential to understand the many cultures that inhabit our planet. One way to really learn about a country is to know how its food tastes. Cooking is the one thing we all have in common. You can prepare a recipe in your kitchen and know that somewhere, perhaps many thousands of miles away, that same dish is probably being prepared in the country where it originated.

Every day in the United States we are reminded of our multicultural richness just by the foods available to us. The delicious result of that abundance is that American cooking has developed into one of the most diverse and appealing cuisines on the planet.

Learning to cook is one of the most important things anybody can do. Cooking skills stay with you your entire life and it sure is fun. Learning to cook takes practice, patience, and common sense, but it's not nuclear science. Cooking certainly has its rewards. Just the simple act of preparing food can lift your spirits. Nothing brings family and friends together better than cooking and then sharing the meal you've made. It can be fun, and you get to eat your mistakes. It can even lead to a high-paying career. Most importantly, you can be proud to say, "Oh, glad you liked it. I did it myself."

Happy cooking!

Matthew Locricchio

Matthew Locricchio

Before You Begin

A Word about Safety

Safety and common sense are the two most important ingredients in any recipe. Before you begin to make the recipes in this book, take a few minutes to master some simple kitchen safety rules.

Ask an adult to be your assistant chef. To ensure your safety, some steps in a recipe are best done with the help of an adult, like handling pots of boiling water or hot cooking oils. Good cooking is about teamwork. With an adult assistant to help, you've got the makings of a perfect team.

Read the entire recipe before you start to prepare it, and have a clear understanding of how the recipe works. If something is not clear, ask your teammate to explain it.

Dress the part of a chef. Wear an apron. Tie back long hair so that it's out of your food and away from open flames. Why not do what a chef does and wear a clean hat to cover your hair!

Always start with clean hands and a clean kitchen before you begin any recipe. Always wash your hands again after handling raw meat, poultry, or fish. Leave the kitchen clean when you're done.

Pot holders and hot pads are your friends. The hands they save may be your own. Use them only if they are dry. Using wet holders on a hot pot can cause a serious burn!

Keep the handles of the pots and pans turned toward the middle of the stove. That way you won't accidentally hit them and knock over pots of hot food. Always use pot holders to open or move a pan on the stove or in the oven.

Remember to turn off the stove and oven when you are finished cooking. Sounds like a simple idea, but it's easy to forget.

Be Sharp about Knives

A simple rule about knife safety is that your hands work as a team. One hand grips the handle and operates the knife while the other guides the food you are cutting. The hand holding the food should never come close to the blade of the knife. Keep the fingertips that hold the food slightly curved and out of the path of the blade, and use your thumb to keep the food steady. Go slowly. There is no reason to rush.

Always hold the knife handle with dry hands. If your hands are wet, the knife might slip.

Work on a cutting board, never a tabletop or countertop.

Never place sharp knives in a sink full of soapy water, where they could be hidden from view. Someone reaching into the water might get hurt.

Greek cooking traces its roots to ancient times, and it remains as popular today as ever. The Greek cook knows that good food comes from ingredients that are fresh and in season. Greece is home to numerous national dishes, which each region skillfully adapts using local ingredients. Local seafood, vegetables, fruits, poultry, and meats all play a role in the richness of Greek regional cooking.

Preparing Greek recipes can be as simple as serving a piece of feta cheese alongside some Greek olives and bread. Or it can involve creating more complex and time-consuming dishes as well. One thing is certain, however, the results are rich and satisfying.

The Greek cook uses a few simple techniques to achieve authentic results in the kitchen. Keep them in mind as you begin to experience the joys of Greek cooking.

Grate

To grate means to finely shred foods. A metal box grater with a handle at the top will give you a place to hold on to as you work. Always be careful when using a grater, and don't allow your fingers to come close to the grating surface.

You can grate dried bread to make bread crumbs, just be sure the grater is not wet. Cucumbers can also be grated into slivers and made into an appetizer such as yogurt and cucumber dip.

Sauté

To lightly fry food in a small amount of fat, butter, or oil, while stirring with a spoon or spatula.

Simmer

To cook food in a liquid at just below the boiling point. Gentle bubbles roll lazily to the top of the liquid that is simmering.

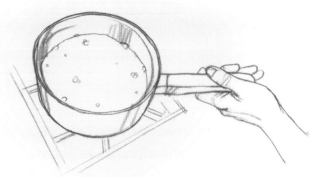

Skim

Fats or impurities will rise to the surface of simmering or boiling soups and sauces. Skimming removes these un-wanted residues while also reducing fat and enriching flavor. Use a large metal spoon or small ladle to scoop off the top layer.

The Regions of Greece and How They Taste

Ancient and modern, rugged and serene, Greece remains the destination of countless travelers who come every year to be a part of the nation's history, beauty, and culture.

Mountains and rugged rock formations cover more than two-thirds of the landmass of Greece. Mount Olympus, the country's tallest mountain, was believed by the ancient Greeks to be the home of the gods. And who would blame them? At almost 10,000 feet (3,048 meters), it dominates not only the surrounding countryside but can be seen from the Aegean Sea.

Greece's culinary history was influenced by the cultures of India and Asia Minor whose trade routes found their way to the Mediterranean Sea. Ships brought new ingredients such as lemons and peaches and the spices cinnamon and nutmeg to Greece. Greek cooks used these exotic ingredients, adding a unique taste to the dishes they prepared.

Greek cooking is a cuisine that also reflects the influence of the holidays that are central to the dominant Greek Orthodox religion. Recipes without meat are prepared during Lent, a time of abstinence and prayer. The arrival of Easter and Christmas prompts great celebrations when special breads, main dishes, and remarkably rich desserts fill the tables.

Greek farmers work hard to coax their crops from the rocky, arid soil. Vegetables such as eggplants, tomatoes, onions, and garlic abound. A large assortment of fruits also enriches the regional cooking of Greece. Sheep and goat farming provides milk to make the staples of the Greek kitchen—yogurt and feta cheese. The fragrance of lemons, oregano, and thyme glides through the air, a hint of some of the flavors waiting to be enjoyed at the next mealtime.

To explore the cooking of Greece we will divide the country into three culinary regions: northern and central Greece, the Peloponnese, and the islands.

NORTH AND CENTRAL

PELOPONNESE

THE ISLANDS

MILES

0   300

BULGARIA

MACEDONIA

ALBANIA

MACEDONIA

THRACE

THESSALONIKI

TURKEY

Mount Olympus

Pindus Mountains

EPIRUS

THESSALY

IONIAN ISLANDS

AEGEAN SEA

LESBOS

CEPHALONIA

IONIAN SEA

Corinth Canal

Taygetus Mtns

NEMEA

ATHENS

ANDROS

PELOPONNESE

Saronic Gulf

CYCLADES

MESSENIA

SPARTA

SPETSES

N

CRETE

MEDITERRANEAN SEA

Northern and Central Greece

Northern Greece forms the southernmost part of the Balkan Peninsula. In the northwest, the region of Epirus borders the Ionian Sea. It is a mountainous place, where rushing rivers and dense forests, filled with deer and wild boar, add to its legendary beauty. Sage and thyme grow among the wealth of wildflowers that help flavor the local honey of Macedonia and neighboring Thrace.

Spring rainfalls are heavy in this part of the country. Sheep and goats graze in the lush mountain pastures of Epirus. Their milk becomes some of the best feta in Greece. The shepherds here have created their own style of cooking over the years that makes great use of local ingredients. A satisfying example is zucchini slow cooked in milk and feta cheese. Another popular Greek cheese called *kefalotyri*, similar to Parmesan, is also produced in the north and used in many regional recipes.

The local dishes bear the influence of the herding culture. Shepherds have had a lasting impact on the cooking of Greece. In the past, shepherds, tending their flocks, traveled with very little cookware. Out of necessity they had to prepare simple, portable meals. One solution was the pita, a savory pie with a wholesome filling baked into a delicate pastry called phyllo (PHE-loh). The clever shepherds found a way to enjoy a delicious meal in the fields, while still keeping a watchful eye on their flocks.

The largest region in Greece is Macedonia, where Alexander the Great once led his armies across the Pindus Mountains. Armies, it is said, travel on their stomachs,

The vibrant colors of dazzling sunflower fields are evident even on a cloudy day in the port city of Thessaloniki.

meaning the soldiers must be well fed if they are expected to march long distances. Alexander's cooks most likely prepared his troops a soup made of lentils, carrots, and onions. High in protein, this hearty dish dates back to ancient Greece and is still a popular part of Macedonian cuisine.

In southern Macedonia, fertile plains give way to the rugged shoreline of the Gulf of Salonika and the Aegean Sea. There you will find Thessaloniki, the second-largest city in Greece and the capital of Macedonia. A port city for more than two thousand years, Thessaloniki, with its shops, outdoor markets, and modern high-rises, is a bustling cosmopolitan city. The many restaurants and tavèrnas, or Greek cafés, specialize in a popular local dish, fresh shrimp baked in tomato and feta cheese sauce.

Macedonia is known for its famous pastries. Regarded as some of the best in Greece, they are as beautiful to look at as they are delicious to eat. Elaborate cream-filled pastries sprinkled with cinnamon and sugar, wrapped in delicate crusts, and baked in wood-burning ovens are sold in local bakeries. Syrup-soaked cakes called *ravani* are made with yogurt. Other cakes are made with farina, a kind of meal made from wheat, and then topped with a sweet, fruit-flavored syrup, which is poured over the cake while it is still hot.

Farther along the peninsula, heading into central Greece, groves of olive trees stand in neat rows on the terraced hillsides. Their green leaves shimmer in the bright sun, fluttering before the clear, blue backdrop of the sky. The locals will tell you there are more than a million olive trees in the region. No wonder Greece is the third-largest producer of olive oil in the world.

Thessaly is another region rich in agriculture and dairy farming. The yogurt and cheese of central Greece rival the best the country has to offer. Potatoes, eggplants, onions, spinach, corn, and beans are among the area's leading crops. The Thessalian cook combines some of these local ingredients into spinach pie, or *spanakopita*, a familiar classic of Greek cooking.

Athens, the capital of Greece, is located at the southern end of the mainland. A city of more than 4.5 million people, it is a place where ancient history and the twenty-first century meet. Tourists flock here to see the ancient ruins and the breathtaking Acropolis—tributes to Greece's glorious past.

Restaurants abound in Athens. An endless variety of both traditional Greek and international restaurants makes this an exciting place to eat. One of the mainstays of any Greek meal is *tzatziki*, a cool cucumber and yogurt dip. It is a great way to beat the legendary summer heat in Athens.

Another dish commonly identified with Greek cooking, *moussakà* is also a common sight on the tabletops of Athens. A combination of eggplant and ground meat baked with cheese in a rich tomato sauce, this popular dish is often served at holiday meals and special celebrations. They say in Greece if you are served moussakà, you must be special because someone went to a lot of trouble to make it for you.

The ingredients for the tzatziki and moussakà served in Athens often come from the central market. Found in the older part of the city, the market dates back to the nineteenth century. It draws thousands of shoppers every day with its stalls of fruits, vegetables, meats, fresh seafood, and poultry. The calls of vendors shouting the praises of their produce fill the air. Athenian shoppers mill about in search of the best cheeses, olives, pickles, garlic, cured meats, and dried fruits.

For a taste of northern and central Greece try: Yogurt and Cucumber Dip; Lentil Soup; Eggplant and Ground Meat Casserole; Chicken and Feta Cheese Pie; Shrimp with Feta Cheese and Tomatoes; Zucchini Simmered in Milk and Feta Cheese; and Yogurt Cake with Fresh Orange Syrup.

The Peloponnese

The Peloponnese, or Peloponnesus as it is sometimes called, is a peninsula separated from mainland Greece by the Corinth Canal. It is shaped like a hand with its fingers pointed toward the waters of the Ionian and Mediterranean seas. Home to some of Greece's most impressive landscapes, it is also a region rich in art and steeped in history and lore.

The original Olympic Games were first held there, appropriately in Olympia, in the central part of the region. The dramatic Taygetus Mountains stretch from the central to the southern Peloponnese. Often snow-capped well into spring, this impressive chain dominates the skyline. In the southeast, the rich soil of Messenia is like an oasis amidst the dry, rocky stretches that cover most of Greece. The land is ideal for olive groves, and Kalamata olive trees grow in abundance here. In fact, the region is responsible for producing thousands of tons of extra-virgin olive oil each year, more than any other place in Greece.

Many of the ingredients essential to the Greek kitchen come from the Peloponnese. Figs, tomatoes, grapes, eggplants, potatoes, artichokes, oregano, and thyme are grown here and highly prized. Lemon and orange groves abound. Roses grown by the monks in the monasteries of the central northern coast are collected and made into a jam sold throughout Greece. The local potatoes are cooked and blended with garlic and ground walnuts to make *skordalia*, a garlic sauce that is served alongside meats, fish, or as an appetizer.

Sparta lies at the eastern base of the Taygetus Mountains. Visitors often stop there before exploring the ruins of Mystra. Many of them take the time to sample the fresh Greek salads of the region. Local romaine lettuce, tomatoes, cucumbers, oregano, feta cheese, and Kalamata olives are tossed together with a dressing of extra-virgin olive oil and vinegar. Fresh and simple, it is yet another delicious way for travelers to get a taste of the best Greece has to offer.

In the Peloponnese town of Nemea, which was once occupied by the Venetians, another classic dish of Hellenic, or Greek, cooking can be found. *Pastitsio*, or baked macaroni and ground meat, is one of the best-known dishes in all of Greek cooking. The Italians probably influenced this dish with its pasta and tomato sauce, but the local Greek cooks have surely made it their own.

For a taste of the Peloponnese try: Baked Macaroni with Cheese and Ground Meat Casserole; Garlic and Potato Sauce; and Greek Salad.

The Islands

Greece's sparkling coastal waters extend from the shores of Turkey to the Ionian Sea, surrounding and separating the some 2,000 islands found there. These islands are the settings of many of the myths and legends central to the ancient people who explored and

Hungry diners will soon fill the tables at this restaurant in Kardumyli, Peloponnese.

settled the region. Even though they were isolated geographically from the rest of the nation, the cuisine and local culture here is just as Greek as that of the mainland.

Just off the southern tip of the first finger of the Peloponnese is the Saronic Gulf and the small island of Spetses, or Spetsni. Home to a legendary pine forest, this tiny island is also famous for its scenic blue-and-white houses nestled above the busy waterfront. Its spectacular beaches make it a popular vacation spot. Cooks here create a local sensation out of fresh fish baked in bread crumbs and a light sauce of delicately flavored tomatoes. This main dish is popular with tourists and locals alike.

Near the western coast of mainland Greece are the Ionian Islands, also known as the Seven Islands. Cephalonia, with its unusual mix of sandy beaches, deep caves, dense forests, and rugged mountains, is a favorite spot for explorers. A local specialty is a creamy feta cheese spread that is served alongside local seafood or as an appetizer.

Zakinthos was called "the flower of the east" by the Venetians, because of its turquoise waters and white cliffs. It remains a major tourist spot today. Local cooks combine potatoes and tomatoes with olives to create a slow-cooked stew called *patates yahni me elies* that would make any vegetarian smile.

The islands of the North Aegean Sea are found off the eastern coast of Greece. These islands have been home to Greeks for thousands of years. Some of Greece's earliest cities were reportedly built there. Among the islands is Lesbos, famous for its olive oil. Its sardines are prized as well. Cured, packed in oil, and sold across the country, they are regarded as the best in Greece.

In the southern waters of the Aegean are the islands of the Cyclades. The brilliant blue sea and sky, spectacular sunsets, bleached white rocks, and bright white houses strung along winding roads closely match the image most people conjure when they think of the Greek islands.

The ancient Greeks chose the name Cyclades, meaning "circle," because the islands form a loose ring. Unlike its drier neighbors, Andros in the north has natural sources of freshwater, so lush vegetable gardens thrive there. One of the island's popular recipes is potatoes oven roasted with lemon juice, olive oil, and oregano and served with local sausages.

The largest and southernmost of all the Greek islands is Crete. More than 150 miles (240 kilometers) of mountains, some of the tallest in Greece, dominate this jagged paradise. According to Greek mythology, it was in a cave on Mount Psiloritis that Zeus, the king of gods, was born. Some islanders still cling to the old ways. This includes traditional clothing and foods. Many of the recipes prepared in Crete today can be traced back to the beginnings of Greek cuisine. Yet it is modern-day industry that is responsible for Crete's healthy economy. The northern coast is home to long stretches of tourist hotels that fill with visitors in the summer months. A popular appetizer in the restaurants of Crete is a salad of tender zucchini topped with a zesty dressing of lemon, olive oil, and oregano. On the southeastern coast, greenhouses grow vegetables, another vital part of the island's economy. The produce raised there is shipped to northern Europe and the drier regions of Greece, where the soil and climate are not ideal for growing tomatoes, eggplants, and cucumbers.

In the coastal town of Agia Galini, the classic recipe of oven-roasted lamb is a specialty. The cooks of Crete prefer the foods they prepare to be simple and delicious. Fresh fruit mixed with yogurt and the local honey is one example of how simple ingredients can yield spectacular results.

For a taste of the islands of Greece try: Baked Fish with Bread Crumbs; Roast Leg of Lamb; Feta Cheese Spread; Tomato, Potato, and Olive Stew; Lemon-Flavored Zucchini; Roasted Potatoes; and Yogurt and Honey with Strawberries.

Now that you have an idea of what makes the cooking of Greece so appealing and delicious, why not give it a try. *Kali orexi*, as the Greeks say—have a good appetite!

The steps of this church provide a breathtaking view of sunset over the islands of the Cyclades.

An assortment of appetizers (meze).

Meze

The great variety and simple, delicate flavors of Greek appetizers are just some of the reasons *mezedes*, or *meze*, are so much a part of the fabric of Greek cuisine. These popular bite-size tidbits have been a part of the cuisine for thousands of years. Some people enjoy them as a complete meal because they are easy to prepare, can be made ahead of time, and make sharing a meal so much fun. You will need to shop for Greek olives, cheeses, and fresh vegetables. The time spent in finding authentic ingredients will be rewarded with a tempting collection of dishes served either hot or cold.

Greek Olive Oil, Olives, and Cheese

Authentic Greek products such as olive oil, olives, and cheeses can be found in supermarkets and specialty stores. Why not try and locate some? Greek olive oil is often less expensive than Italian or French and can be a good buy without sacrificing flavor. Greek olives have a bold flavor and a unique aroma. Other than feta, Greek cheeses may be a little more difficult to find. Check to see if there is a Mediterranean or Middle Eastern market in your area that specializes in imported Greek foods.

Olive Oil

With so many olive groves spread over the hillsides, it is no surprise that Greece produces thousands of tons of olive oil each year. The oils are rich and dark, with the best ones coming from Crete and Kalamata, where the climate is ideal for growing olives. There are many varieties and grades of olive oil. Cold-pressed, extra-virgin oil comes from the first pressing, or crushing, of the olives without the use of high heat or the addition of extra water. This means the oil has a low acidity, less than 1 percent, and therefore great flavor. Many people regard cold-pressed as the best of the extra-virgin olive oils. When you get your olive oil home, store it in a cool place, away from bright sunlight.

Olives

Kalamatas

These olives are cured in salt, vinegar, and olive oil. Curing means ripening the olives, which are firm and bitter when they are first picked. They are then placed in a salty liquid where they mellow in flavor for a few months as they ripen. Then olive oil and vinegar are added to complete the curing. The result is a soft, purple, and almond-shaped olive that is plump and meaty. The skin is smooth, and the flesh is firm. The flavor of Kalamatas is strong. They are often used in stuffing or crushed into bread dough and baked. Kalamata olives are also used in salads, main dishes, and as appetizers. They can be found packed in jars in the specialty section of most supermarkets or sold in bulk in import stores.

Throumbes

You have probably seen these olives and not known they were Greek. They look like tiny prunes because their skin is black and wrinkled. Their flavor can be quite strong, though some varieties are sweet. This is an excellent olive to eat on its own or to add to a Greek salad. Just remind your guests to remove the pits.

Cracked Green Olives

These large olives are picked before they ripen. The olive is then cracked open with a stone, allowing it to absorb the salt water in which it is cured. The pits of cracked green olives are easy to remove, so the olives are easy to chop.

Cheese

Feta

Feta is a fresh white cheese that is soft and crumbly. Check to see where the cheese you are buying was produced. Feta produced in Greece is made from goat's or sheep's milk. You can buy it whole or crumbled.

Kefalotyri

This hard grating cheese is imported from Greece and made from sheep's milk. It may be difficult to find outside of a Greek specialty market. Parmesan or pecorino Romano cheeses are excellent substitutes as both cheeses are similar in flavor and texture.

Greek-Style Yogurt *Yaourti*

Yogurt is an essential part of many Greek recipes. It adds a distinctive, rich, and refreshing flavor. If you can find yogurt made from sheep's or goat's milk, use it in the recipes that follow to get an authentic Greek flavor. If not, here is a recipe to make your own version of Greek-style yogurt. You might be surprised at how delicious yogurt can taste.

Makes 1 cup

Ingredients

2 10-inch squares of cheesecloth

2 cups plain yogurt (not low fat)

1 metal hand strainer (see illustration)

1 large glass or ceramic bowl

On your mark, get set, strain!

- Place the squares of cheesecloth into the hand strainer over the bowl as shown in the illustration.

- Carefully pour in the yogurt.

- Set the bowl in the refrigerator and let the yogurt strain for about 2 to 3 hours. The yogurt will reduce to about 1 cup.

- Once the liquid has drained, lift the cheesecloth out of the strainer and spoon the thickened yogurt into a clean bowl.

- Cover the bowl and return it to the refrigerator until ready to use.

Chef's Tip

The liquid that collects into the bowl is called whey. You can discard the whey, or you can chill it, place it in a blender with fresh fruit, and make a smoothie. It is healthy and tastes good, too!

Yogurt and Cucumber Dip
Tzatziki

With the hot summer months in Athens refreshing light dishes are the rule. This dip combines crunchy cucumbers and cool yogurt blended with fresh mint and dill. Tzatziki is made in Athenian restaurants as well as in kitchens throughout Greece. Serve it with an assortment of Greek olives, feta cheese, and crusty bread for the perfect light summertime meal.

Serves 6

Ingredients

1 large cucumber

1 clove garlic

2 to 3 sprigs fresh mint

2 to 3 sprigs fresh dill

3 tablespoons extra-virgin olive oil (preferably Greek)

1 tablespoon white vinegar

1 cup Greek-style yogurt (page 25) or 1 ½ cups plain yogurt (not low fat)

1 teaspoon salt

freshly ground black pepper to taste

On your mark, get set, chill!

- Wash and peel the cucumber.
- Grate the cucumber, using the largest holes on a box grater, into a bowl large enough to hold all the ingredients.
- Place the grated cucumber into a hand strainer over the sink.
- Using the back of a large spoon, gently press down and squeeze out the excess liquid.
- Let the cucumber drain for a minute or two and then return the cucumber to the bowl.
- Peel and chop the garlic and add to the cucumbers.
- Wash the mint and dill and shake off the excess water.
- Remove the mint leaves from the stems.
- Finely chop the mint, measure 1 to 1 ½ tablespoons, and add to the bowl.
- Chop the dill, measure 1 to 1 ½ tablespoons, and add to the bowl.

- Add the olive oil, vinegar, yogurt, salt, and pepper, and stir gently to combine all the ingredients.
- Chill at least 1 hour before serving.

Chef's Tip

If you don't have a box grater, cut the peeled cucumber in half lengthwise. Using a teaspoon, start at one end and scrape out the seeds, discarding them when you are done. Cut the cucumber into ¼-inch chunks and place in a bowl then continue with the recipe.

Garlic and Potato Sauce
Skordalia

A sauce made from garlic and potatoes? Even though it may sound strange, just wait until you taste how its delicate flavors combine to create one of Greece's best-known sauces. Garlic and potato sauce can be found as a spread on a table of appetizers as well as alongside fish or meat dishes. Many different versions of this dish using local ingredients are popular throughout the country. This version comes from the Peloponnese.

Serves 4 to 6

Ingredients

4 quarts water

1 tablespoon salt

4 to 5 medium-size red-skinned or white potatoes (about 1 to 1 ½ pounds)

4 garlic cloves

½ cup extra-virgin olive oil (preferably Greek)

½ cup chopped almonds or walnuts

2 tablespoons fresh lemon juice

1 teaspoon salt

sesame crackers or crusty bread for serving

On your mark, get set, cook!

- Peel the potatoes. Cut them in half, then into 2-inch chunks.

- Bring the water, potatoes, and salt to a boil in a covered pot. Cover the pot with the lid slightly ajar and cook 12 to 15 minutes or until soft and tender.

- Crush, peel, and chop the garlic, and set aside.

- Ask your adult assistant to help you drain the potatoes.

- Return the potatoes to the pot and place them over low heat for a minute or two. This will help dry any excess liquid left over from the cooking.

- Turn off the heat and cover the pot.

- Place the garlic, olive oil, nuts, lemon juice, and salt in a blender, in that order.

- Press the lid firmly into place and blend at low speed for 5 seconds.

- Now blend at high speed for 30 seconds, or until smooth.

- Turn off the blender and pour the blended oil mixture into a bowl.

- Remove the lid from the potatoes and add one-third of the blended oil.

- Mash well with a potato masher or large spoon to combine.

- Add another third of the oil and continue to mash, making sure to combine all ingredients.

- Add the remaining third of the oil to the potatoes and mash until you have a smooth paste.

- Using a spoon, whip together all the ingredients into a smooth mixture that is firm enough to keep its shape when you scoop it up in a spoon.

- Taste it to decide if it needs more salt and add some if necessary.

- Chill thoroughly. Serve with sesame crackers or crusty bread.

Greek Salad *Horiatiki Salata*

Why has this collection of delicious greens, tomatoes, herbs, and feta won the hearts of diners for countless years? Because it's just plain delicious! The hardest thing about preparing this salad is finding the freshest vegetables. The tomatoes should be firm and fully ripe and, if possible, the dried oregano should be Greek. Follow this recipe from Sparta, complete with an authentic Greek salad dressing, and see why the popular salads of this beautiful country have such a devoted following.

Serves 4 to 6

Ingredients

SALAD

3 to 4 medium-size ripe tomatoes

1 cucumber

1 medium-size red onion

1 green bell pepper

1 medium-size head of romaine lettuce

6 to 8 ounces feta cheese

1 teaspoon dried oregano (preferably Greek)

10 to 12 Kalamata or other black olives

2 or 3 anchovies (optional)

DRESSING

⅓ cup extra-virgin olive oil (preferably Greek)

1 tablespoon red wine vinegar

½ teaspoon salt

freshly ground pepper to taste

On your mark, get set, toss!

- Wash the tomatoes, cut out and discard the stem circle at the top, and cut the tomatoes into wedges. Place them in a salad bowl large enough to hold all the ingredients.

- Wash and peel the cucumbers. Slice them in half lengthwise and then cut them into ½-inch-thick slices. Add to the salad bowl with the tomatoes.

- Peel and cut the red onion in half. Cut each half into thin slices and add to the bowl.

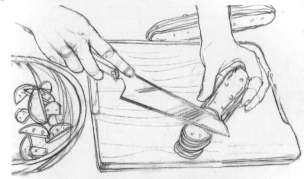

- Wash the green bell pepper and cut in half. Remove the seeds and discard. Cut each half into small chunks and add to the bowl.

- Separate the romaine leaves from the stem. Wash with cold water to remove any dirt. Shake off excess water and pat dry with paper towels.

- Tear the lettuce into bite-size pieces and lay them on a few sheets of paper towel.

- Sprinkle the oregano over the ingredients in the salad bowl. Use your very clean hands, a large spoon and fork, or salad tongs to combine all the ingredients.

- Lay the lettuce pieces on a serving platter.

- Using a fork, blend together the ingredients for the salad dressing in a small bowl.

- Pour the dressing over the ingredients in the salad bowl. Toss to coat the ingredients, and arrange the dressed vegetables over the lettuce.

- Arrange the olives on the salad.

- Add the feta cheese.

- Add the anchovies, if you are using them, and serve immediately.

Feta Cheese Spread
Pretza me Psomi

The most famous Greek cheese is feta. It is made in different varieties all over Greece. This spread will give you a taste of the island of Cephalonia. Serve it as an appetizer with plenty of crusty bread or crispy sesame crackers. You can also use it as a dip for fresh vegetables.

Serves 4 to 6

Ingredients

1 ½ cups of crumbled feta cheese

½ cup ricotta cheese or sour cream

¼ cup Greek-style yogurt (page 25) or plain yogurt

3 tablespoons extra-virgin olive oil (preferably Greek)

1 teaspoon dried oregano (preferably Greek) or thyme

2 ripe tomatoes

1 loaf crusty French or Italian bread or sesame flatbreads

extra olive oil for drizzling

On your mark, get set, serve!

- Place the feta in a bowl large enough to hold all the ingredients except for the tomatoes.

- Add the ricotta or sour cream, yogurt, olive oil, and oregano or thyme.

- Using an electric hand mixer, blend on low speed for 30 seconds until smooth and spreadable.

- Chill the spread for at least 1 hour.

- When ready to serve, chop the tomatoes into small chunks and place them in a separate serving bowl.

- Serve the spread with the sliced bread or sesame flatbreads, chopped tomatoes, and extra olive oil to drizzle on top.

Lemon-Flavored Zucchini
Kolokithakia Vrasta

Here is another perfect dish to add to your collection of appetizers. It is served in Crete as a popular salad along with other assorted *meze*.

Serves 4 to 6

Ingredients

3 medium-size zucchini

¼ cup extra-virgin olive oil (preferably Greek) plus 2 tablespoons

1 lemon

½ teaspoon oregano (preferably Greek)

1 teaspoon salt

freshly ground black pepper

1 cup water plus 3 tablespoons

crusty bread or sesame crackers for serving

On your mark, get set . . .

- Wash the skin of the zucchini carefully with a vegetable brush to remove any sand.

- Combine the olive oil, juice of ½ of the lemon, oregano, and the salt and pepper, in a small bowl and set aside.

Cook!

- Preheat the oven to 375°F.

- Place a vegetable steamer in the bottom of a 4-to-6 quart pan. Pour in the cup of water. Lay the zucchini on the steamer, cover the pan, and bring to a boil over medium-high heat.

- Reduce the heat to simmer and cook for 3 to 4 minutes.

- Remove the zucchini from the steamer and allow it to cool enough to handle comfortably.

- Cut the zucchini in half lengthwise, then cut each half lengthwise, again. You should end up with 4 long thin spears.

- Lay the spears in a small baking pan just large enough to hold them without crowding.

- Add the 3 tablespoons of water to the bottom of the baking pan and pour the olive oil mixture over the zucchini.

- Cover with aluminum foil and bake for 5 minutes. Set a timer so you don't forget.

- After 5 minutes reduce the oven to 325°F. Bake for 30 minutes or until the zucchini are just tender. Once or twice during the baking remove the foil and baste the zucchini with the juices from the pan. You can add a little extra water if needed.

- Remove the zucchini from the oven and let cool for at least 10 to 15 minutes. Pour the liquid in the bottom of the pan into a small bowl and set aside.

- Cut the spears into ¼ pieces and place in a serving bowl.

- Pour the cooking liquid over the zucchini.

- Serve cold or at room temperature with crusty bread or sesame crackers.

Egg and lemon soup with chicken (left) and lentil soup (center).

Chicken Stock
Zoumi apo Katopaulo

It is quicker and more convenient perhaps to buy canned chicken broth. Homemade chicken stock, however, tastes better because it is freshly made. If you have never made your own, this is the perfect chance. As any Greek cook will tell you, nothing is as rich tasting and satisfying as home cooking. Use this recipe when making egg and lemon soup with chicken (page 40) or as a light broth to enjoy on its own.

Makes 2 quarts

Ingredients

3 to 4 whole cloves

1 large onion (unpeeled)

1 carrot

1 stalk celery

3 ½ pounds cut-up chicken (preferably organic)

3 quarts cold water

On your mark, get set . . .

- Firmly sink the pointed ends of the cloves into the brown outer skin of the onion.

- Wash the carrot and celery but don't peel them.

- Rinse the chicken under running water.

Cook!

- Place the chicken and the rest of the ingredients into a 4- to 6-quart pot.

- Add the water and bring to a boil; this will take about 20 to 30 minutes. As the liquid starts to boil, use a large spoon to skim off and discard any foam or fat that may rise to the top.

- Cover the pot, leaving the lid slightly ajar. Reduce the heat to low and simmer for 1 ½ to 2 hours. As it cooks, continue to skim the stock as needed.

- Turn off the heat. Ask your adult assistant to strain the broth through a metal colander into a heatproof bowl or pan.

- Discard the vegetables. Save the chicken for another recipe.

- Allow the stock to cool for about 20 minutes. Then cover and refrigerate it.

- After the stock is chilled, remove and discard the fat that has separated and risen to the top.

- The stock will keep in the refrigerator for up to three days, or you can freeze it for up to six months.

Egg and Lemon Soup with Chicken
Avgolemono Soupa

This soup is very popular all over Greece. Kids and adults love it and once you try it, it's one soup you're not soon going to forget. It is made from lemon and eggs that combine into one of the basic sauces in Greek cooking, called *avgolemono*.

Serves 4 to 6

Ingredients

2 lemons

1 bunch fresh mint or 1 teaspoon dried

¾ cup cooked chicken (recipe on page 38)

8 cups homemade or canned chicken or vegetable stock or water

½ cup medium-or long-grained rice

1 teaspoon salt

3 medium eggs

On your mark, get set . . .

- Cut the lemons in half, squeeze and strain the juice into a small bowl.

- Wash the fresh mint and remove the leaves. Discard the stems. Chop the mint leaves, measure 2 tablespoons, and set aside.

- Cut the chicken into small cubes, measure ½ cup, and set aside.

Cook!

- Bring the stock or water to a boil over high heat.

- Slowly add the rice. Cover the pot, reduce the heat to simmer and cook for 12 to 15 minutes.

- Add the salt and chicken, and continue to simmer uncovered as you prepare the egg-and-lemon sauce.

- Beat the eggs in a large bowl with an electric mixer for about 2 minutes.

- Add the lemon juice. Beat for another 30 seconds until light and foamy.

- Turn off the mixer and remove the beater.

- Slowly ladle ½ cup of the simmering soup into the egg-and-lemon sauce.

- Add another ½ cup of the soup to the mixture and continue stirring constantly.

- Pour the egg-and-lemon sauce into the remaining soup and stir well.

- Don't let the soup boil or it will curdle, so keep the temperature low.

- Cook for 3 to 4 minutes stirring often.

- Add the chopped mint and serve hot.

Lentil Soup *Faki*

Let's be honest. Lentils are not the most exciting of foods to look at. Appearances, however, can be deceiving. In Greece the lentil has been the food of kings and commoners alike for thousands of years. This little legume is packed with protein and exceptional flavor. A hot bowl of lentil soup can be deeply satisfying. Here is an easy-to-make lentil soup that is vegetarian. It will fill your kitchen with a delicious aroma as it simmers on the stove. Why not give it a try?

Serves 6 to 8

Ingredients

16 ounces (2 cups) dried lentils

2 medium-size onions

2 carrots

1 pound fresh plum tomatoes or 1 15-ounce can chopped tomatoes with their liquid

5 to 6 sprigs of flat-leaf parsley

2 garlic cloves

¼ cup extra-virgin olive oil (preferably Greek)

¼ cup red wine vinegar

1 whole bay leaf

1 teaspoon dried oregano (preferably Greek)

2 teaspoons salt

½ teaspoon freshly ground black pepper

8 cups water

On your mark . . .

- Pour the lentils onto a baking tray. Check the lentils carefully for little stones or anything that is not a lentil and remove.

- Place the dried lentils in a bowl and cover with cold water. Stir the lentils with your hands and then let them fall to the bottom of the bowl. Remove any that float on the surface.

- Pour into a hand strainer and rinse with cold water. Set aside to drain.

Get set . . .

- Peel the onions and chop into medium-size chunks.

- Wash and peel the carrots and chop into 2-inch pieces.

- Remove the stem circle from the top of the tomatoes, coarsely chop the tomatoes, and place in a bowl. If using canned tomatoes, measure 1 cup with some of the liquid and set aside.

- Wash the parsley and shake off the excess water. Coarsely chop.

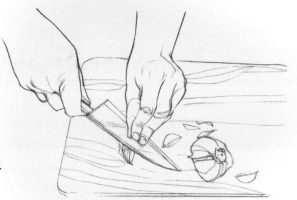

- Slightly crush the garlic by laying the flat side of a chef's knife on the clove and pressing firmly to break open the skin. Remove the skin and chop the garlic and set aside.

Cook!

- In a pot large enough to hold all the ingredients (6 to 8 quarts), heat the olive oil over low heat for about 30 seconds.

- Add the onions and sauté for 4 to 5 minutes, or until they change from white to almost clear.

- Add the carrots and sauté for another 4 to 5 minutes.

- Add the tomatoes, parsley, garlic, red wine vinegar, bay leaf, oregano, salt, pepper, and water. Turn the heat to medium and bring to a boil. This will take about 15 minutes.

- Add the lentils and stir well to combine.

- Cover the pot, reduce the heat to low, and cook for 1 hour, or until the lentils and carrots are tender.

- During cooking, skim any foam that rises to the top with a large spoon or ladle and discard.

- Before serving, taste the soup and decide if it needs more salt or pepper. You may also need to add a little extra water if the soup is too thick.

- Serve hot.

Chef's Tip

This soup will thicken the day after it is prepared. You can add more water to it when you reheat it, or you can serve the lentils as a side dish to go along with roast leg of lamb (page 79).

Potato, tomato, and olive stew (left)
and roasted potatoes (right).

Tomato, Potato, and Olive Stew
Patates Yahni me Elies

The potato is a newcomer to Greek cuisine. The story of how the potato made its way into the kitchens of Greece has become a culinary legend. Early in the nineteenth century, a clever government official came up with a plan to give potatoes to the population. The skeptical Greeks could not be persuaded to give them a try. So the official filled baskets with the mysterious tubers and placed them near the harbor. He left strict orders that the potatoes were not to be touched, or the thief would face dire consequences. The sun rose the next day to reveal the baskets—empty! It seemed the potato had found a home in Greece. Give this recipe from the island of Zakynthos in the Ionian Sea a try. But don't steal the potatoes!

Serves 6

Ingredients

2 pounds small red-skinned or Yukon gold potatoes

1 medium-size onion

2 garlic cloves

½ pound Kalamata olives

¼ teaspoon dried red pepper flakes

1 teaspoon dried oregano (preferably Greek)

1 28-ounce can chopped tomatoes with their liquid

1 small bunch flat-leaf parsley

⅓ cup extra-virgin olive oil (preferably Greek)

2 tablespoons red wine vinegar

On your mark, get set . . .

- Peel the potatoes and cut them in quarters. Put the potatoes in a bowl and cover with cold water.

- Peel the onion and cut into thin slices, measure 1 ½ cups and set aside.

- Slightly crush the garlic by laying the flat side of a chef's knife on the clove and pressing evenly to break open the skin. Remove the skin and chop the garlic and set aside.

- Pit the olives if they are not already pitted. To do this, lay a few at a time on a cutting board and using the flat side of a chef's knife, press down on the olive. Remove the pit and discard. Roughly chop the olives, measure 1 cup, and set aside.

- Combine the dried red pepper flakes and the oregano and set aside.

- Measure 2 cups of canned tomatoes, with the liquid, and set aside.

- Wash the parsley and shake well to remove excess water. Chop the parsley, measure ½ cup, and refrigerate.

Cook!

- Preheat the oven to 375°F.

- Place a 10- or 12-inch frying pan over medium-high heat and add the olive oil. After about 30 seconds, add the potatoes and sauté for 5 minutes, or until they begin to turn brown.

- Remove the potatoes with a metal slotted spoon to a medium-size bowl, keeping the oil in the pan.

- Return the frying pan to the stovetop, lower the heat to medium and add the onions.

- Cook for 3 to 4 minutes or until the onions are soft.

- Add the red wine vinegar, garlic, red pepper flakes, oregano, tomatoes, and olives. Cook for 3 to 4 minutes, then turn off the heat.

- Arrange the potatoes in a single layer in an ovenproof baking dish.

- Spoon the tomato mixture evenly over the top and bake uncovered for 45 minutes, or until the potatoes are tender.

- When ready to serve, sprinkle with the chopped parsley, and serve hot.

Roasted Potatoes
Patates Riganates

When potatoes are roasted in the oven, they absorb the flavor of whatever is cooking with them. Nobody knows this better than the Greek cook. This recipe comes from the island of Andros, in the Cyclades, where potatoes are plucked from the rich volcanic soil and turned into a variety of dishes. It is the perfect dish to serve with roast leg of lamb (page 79), baked fish with bread crumbs (page 68), or just as a delicious side dish when you want to impress your guests.

Serves 6

Ingredients

3 pounds Idaho or russet baking potatoes

⅓ cup extra-virgin olive oil (preferably Greek) plus 1 teaspoon for coating the baking pan

2 garlic cloves

1 to 2 lemons

1 teaspoon salt

2 teaspoons dried oregano (preferably Greek)

freshly ground black pepper

½ cup chicken stock or water

On your mark, get set . . .

- Preheat the oven to 400°F.

- Peel the potatoes. Cut them in half lengthwise and lay them, flat side down, on the cutting board.

- Cut each half into long slices about ½ inch wide.

- Cut the slices into 1- to 1 ½-inch cubes.

- Place the cut potatoes into a large bowl.

- Add the olive oil and toss well with a spoon to coat the potatoes with the oil.

- Slightly crush the garlic by laying the flat side of a chef's knife on the clove and pressing evenly to break open the skin. Remove the skin, chop the garlic, and add to the bowl.

- Cut the lemon in half and squeeze out the juice through a small hand strainer to catch any seeds.

- Measure 1/3 cup lemon juice and add to the potatoes.

- Now add the salt, dried oregano, and black pepper.

- Toss well to combine all the ingredients.

Cook!

- Lightly coat a 13 x 9-inch baking pan with a teaspoon of olive oil. An ovenproof glass or metal pan will work best.

- Place the potatoes in the pan and spread them evenly into a single layer with a spoon.

- Pour the stock or water over the potatoes, place pan in the oven, and bake the potatoes for 30 minutes.

- Open the oven door and, using a spatula or metal spoon, give the potatoes a stir. If they seem too dry, add a little more stock or liquid, but no more than 1/3 cup.

- Close the oven door and roast the potatoes another 30 minutes. They should be golden brown and tender.

- Serve hot.

Zucchini Simmered in Milk and Feta Cheese
Kolokythakia sto Gala

The northwestern region of Epirus, in the shadows of the Pindus Mountains, is rich with history, and known for its shepherd's cuisine. Large amounts of rain produce pastures that provide excellent grazing for the goats and sheep who feed on it and the milk from the region is prized. Many believe the feta cheese from there is some of the best in the country. The traditional recipes here are simple and basic, but remarkably delicious. Try this one alongside baked fish with bread crumbs (page 68). Here's a great example of how good simple Greek cooking can be.

Serves 4

Ingredients

6 green onions

6 to 8 sprigs of Italian flat-leaf parsley plus extra for garnish

4 zucchini (about 1 ½ pounds)

½ teaspoon salt

½ pound Greek feta cheese

2 tablespoons salted butter

2 tablespoons extra-virgin olive oil (preferably Greek)

1 ½ cup whole milk

¼ teaspoon ground nutmeg

On your mark . . .

- Wash the green onions. Remove the root end and any dark leaves. Chop them, both the white part and about 3 to 4 inches of the green sections, into small pieces and set aside.

- Wash the parsley, shake off the excess water, chop, measure ½ cup, and set aside.

- Wash the zucchini very well to remove any sand, then cut into ¼-inch slices, measure about 4 cups, and set aside.

Get set . . .

- Crumble the feta cheese into small chunks into a bowl and set aside.

Cook!

- In a 4-to-5 quart saucepan melt the butter and olive oil together over medium heat.

- Add the green onions and parsley and cook uncovered for 8 to 10 minutes or until the onions are soft. Stir frequently to evenly cook the onions.

- Add the zucchini and salt and carefully stir the zucchini well to combine with the onions.

- Continue to cook at a soft boil for 6 to 8 minutes or until most of the liquid in the pan has cooked away. If the pan begins to boil too fast, lower the heat.

- Add the feta cheese and mix well.

- Cook for 3 minutes or until the feta has melted.

- Add the milk, reduce the heat to low, and continue to cook uncovered for 10 minutes or until the milk has been absorbed and the sauce is thick.

- Garnish with fresh chopped parsley and serve hot or at room temperature.

Spinach pie (left) and chicken and feta cheese pie (center).

Spinach Pie *Spanakopita*

Fresh spinach blends with feta to create the most famous of all Greek dishes. This recipe will introduce you to phyllo dough, a common pastry in many Greek kitchens and available frozen in most supermarkets and specialty food stores. Follow the package directions for thawing and preparing the phyllo so that you will be ready to start when it is time to make the recipe. To make the spinach pie open faced, as pictured on page 52, just leave off the top two layers of phyllo dough as indicated in the recipe.

Serves 6 to 8

Ingredients

1 ½ pounds fresh spinach (preferably organic)

4 green onions

1 small bunch flat-leaf parsley (about 10 stems)

1 small bunch fresh dill or fresh mint

2 leeks

½ cup extra-virgin olive oil plus 2 tablespoons (preferably Greek)

¼ teaspoon salt

3 large eggs

8 ounces (1 ½ cups) feta cheese

12 sheets phyllo dough, completely thawed

2 tablespoons softened butter plus 1 tablespoon for greasing the pan

On your mark . . .

- Fill a clean sink with cold water.

- Separate the leaves of the spinach and drop them into the water. Let them soak for a few minutes, gently moving them around with your hands to help dislodge any dirt.

- Carefully lift the spinach into a colander, being careful not to disturb the water too much. Drain the water from the sink and clean any dirt or sand from the bottom.

- Refill the sink with cold water and repeat the washing at least once. If there is still sand or dirt in the sink, repeat a final time. Drain the spinach and roughly chop.

- Return the chopped spinach to the colander.

Get set . . .

- Wash the green onions. Remove the root end and any dark leaves. Chop them, both the white part and about 3 to 4 inches of the green sections, into small pieces. Measure ½ cup and set aside.

- Wash the parsley, shake off the excess water, chop, measure ½ cup, and set aside.

- Chop the dill or mint, measure 2 tablespoons, and set aside.

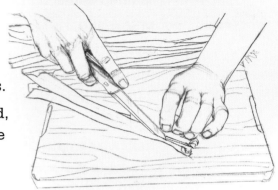

- Cut off the root end of the leeks and discard any brown or damaged leaves.

- Place the leeks on a cutting board and, using the tip of a sharp knife, slice the leek in half lengthwise.

- Wash each half carefully under cold water, spreading the leaves apart with your fingers to separate the layers. Rinse out any sand that may be trapped. Repeat with the other half.

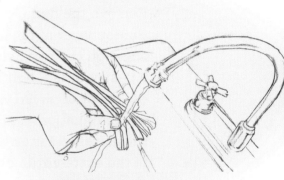

- Slice the white section and about 1 inch of the pale green section into thin slices and set aside.

- Combine ¼ cup of the olive oil and 1 tablespoon softened butter and set aside in a small bowl. In a separate bowl, combine the remaining ¼ cup of olive oil and 1 tablespoon softened butter, and set aside.

Cook!

- Preheat the oven to 350°F.

- Heat ¼ cup of the olive oil-butter mixture in a 12-inch skillet for about 30 seconds.

- Add the leeks and green onions and sauté for 5 to 7 minutes.

- Add the spinach and salt. Carefully sauté for another 5 to 7 minutes.

- After it has cooked, the spinach will have given off a lot of liquid.

Pour it into the colander to drain. Using the back of a large spoon gently press on the spinach to extract the liquid. Let it cool for 10 to 15 minutes.

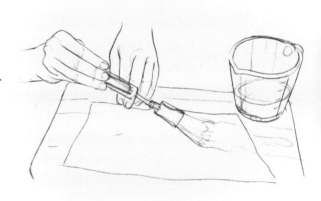

- In a large bowl, combine the feta, beaten eggs, chopped dill or mint, and the drained spinach mixture.

- Mix well to combine all the ingredients and refrigerate. This is the pie filling.

- Butter the bottom and sides of a 12 x 9 x 3-inch baking dish or a 10-inch pie dish with the extra tablespoon of butter.

- Remove the phyllo from the refrigerator and take out the number of sheets you will need plus two extra. Cover the sheets with a clean damp cloth to keep them from drying out.

- Rewrap any leftover phyllo you won't be using and refrigerate or refreeze.

- Remove the damp cloth from the top layer of phyllo. Place one sheet on the work surface. With a pastry brush, lightly spread the sheet of phyllo with a butter-oil combination: 1 tablespoon of the softened butter and ¼ cup of the extra-virgin olive oil. This step will make sure your pastry is flaky and will keep the layers from sticking together.

- Carefully lift the oiled sheet and place it in the pie dish. Press the pastry gently into the bottom and sides of the pie dish to reduce the chance of tearing. Don't worry if the phyllo tears a little. Let the rest of the pastry hang over the outside of the baking dish for now; you will trim it later.

- Spread the next layer of phyllo with the oil and butter combination.

- Carefully lift it and place it on top of the previous sheet.

- Repeat the brushing and layering of phyllo until you have a total of 8 layers.

- Cover the remaining sheets with the damp cloth.

- Remove the pie filling from the refrigerator.

- Scoop the filling out of the bowl with a slotted spoon to drain off any excess liquid, and spread the filling evenly over the pastry.

- Brush the final two sheets with the oil-butter mixture and place them on top of the filling. This is the top crust of the pie. Now trim the hanging pastry edges to about 3 inches in length—a pair of kitchen scissors or a sharp paring knife works well for this.

- Working with one at a time, carefully lift the corners of the overhanging pastry and roll up the edges to the top of the pie dish to form a crust. Be patient, this is a slow process.

- Using a sharp knife, make some slits in the top crust of the pie to help the steam escape as the pie bakes.

- Bake for 40 to 45 minutes until golden brown and crispy. Let cool 15 minutes.

- Serve warm or cold, sliced in squares or wedges.

Chicken and Feta Cheese Pie
Kotopita me Feta

This dish comes from Crete. It is a perfect meal for all seasons because it can be enjoyed hot or cold. Try serving it with a Greek salad (page 31). This recipe calls for phyllo dough but you can also use a frozen pie shell with a top crust. Just follow the package instructions for thawing the phyllo or pie shell. Once you try it, you will be making this recipe again and again.

Serves 6

Ingredients

2 boneless chicken breasts, 8 to 10 ounces total (preferably organic)

1 bunch green onions

2 stalks celery

1 small bunch fresh dill

HERB MIX

½ teaspoon dried tarragon

½ teaspoon dried oregano (preferably Greek)

½ teaspoon dried mint

½ teaspoon dried thyme

1 pinch freshly ground black pepper

2 eggs

10 sheets phyllo dough, fully thawed, or 1 10-inch frozen pie crust with top crust, fully thawed

3 ounces (¾ cup) feta cheese

½ cup grated pecorino Romano cheese, about 2 ounces

⅓ cup extra-virgin olive oil (preferably Greek)

1 tablespoon softened butter plus extra for the baking pan

On your mark, get set . . .

- Cut each chicken breast lengthwise into 1-inch-wide slices. Cut the slices into 1-inch cubes and place in a large bowl.

- Thoroughly wash the cutting board where the chicken was cut, the knife, and your hands with hot soapy water.

- Wash the green onions and remove the root end along with any discolored outer leaves. Cut into ¼-inch slices. Measure ¾ cup and add to the chicken cubes.

- Wash and dice the celery into small chunks, measure ¾ cup, and add to the chicken.
- Wash the dill and shake off any excess water. Separate the feathery tops from the stems. Discard the stems. Chop the dill, measure ½ cup, and add to the chicken.
- Combine the herb mix in a small bowl. Add to the chicken mixture.
- Crumble the feta cheese into the mixture. Add the pecorino Romano cheese and 2 tablespoons of the olive oil, and mix well.
- Break the eggs into the bowl with the chicken mixture and mix well with a spoon to combine all the ingredients. This is the chicken pie filling.
- Refrigerate the filling while you prepare the rest of the recipe.

Cook!

- Preheat the oven to 350°F.
- If using a frozen pie crust: Place the cooled filling in the crust. Add the top crust. Place the pie on the middle rack of the oven and bake for 50 to 55 minutes, or until the top is golden brown.
- Remove the pie from the oven to a cooling rack. Let it cool for 10 to 15 minutes before slicing and serving. The pie dish can also be served cold.
- If using phyllo pastry: Lightly butter a 9- or 10-inch pie dish and set aside.
- Melt the butter over low heat. When the butter stops bubbling, add the olive oil and stir to combine. Remove the pan from the stove and pour the butter-oil mixture into a heatproof bowl and set aside.
- Remove the phyllo from the refrigerator and count out 10 sheets. Carefully lift the sheets and lay them on the countertop or work surface, then cover with a clean damp cloth.
- Reroll the unused sheets, wrap them well and refrigerate or refreeze.
- Have the butter and oil mixture close by.
- Remove the damp cloth.
- Using a pastry brush, lightly spread the surface of the dough with a thin coating of the olive oil and butter combination. Take your time so you do not tear the dough, though it's all right if you do.

- Carefully lift the sheet of the phyllo and lay it in the pie dish. Gently press it into the sides and corners. Let the rest of the pastry hang down evenly around the sides of the pie dish.

- Repeat this step of brushing each sheet of phyllo with the oil-butter mixture and carefully laying it on top of the previous one.

- Don't lay the phyllo sheets directly on top of each other. Stagger them so they more evenly cover the whole pie dish. That way, when you fold them over the filling, they will create a top crust to cover the filling.

- After you have brushed and layered 8 sheets of phyllo, it is time to finish the pie.

- Remove the filling from the refrigerator. Spread the filling evenly on top of the phyllo sheets. Smooth the surface with a spoon to make sure the filling is even.

- Carefully lift one corner of a sheet of the overhanging pastry and lay it on top of the pie filling. Continue lifting the remaining edges to create the top crust of the pie. Tuck in any edges to prevent them from burning.

- Brush the top of the pie with any remaining oil-butter mixture to cover any spots you may have missed. Don't worry if the entire surface of the filling is not covered.

- Sprinkle the finished pie with a few drops of cold water.

- Place on the middle rack of the oven and bake for 50 to 55 minutes, or until the top is golden brown and crispy.

- Remove the pie dish from the oven to a cooling rack. Let it cool for 10 to 15 minutes before slicing and serving. This dish can also be served cold.

Eggplant and ground meat casserole.

Eggplant and Ground Meat Casserole
Moussaka

This famous dish uses two recipes common in Greek cooking. One is a ground meat filling, and the other is a French sauce, called béchamel. There are lots of steps to this recipe, so if you don't have a lot of time, this is probably not the dish to make. It may be more involved than most recipes, but the results are worth every bit of effort you put into it.

Serves 6

Ingredients

1 firm large eggplant

2 tablespoons salt

GROUND MEAT FILLING

2 small white onions

1 garlic clove

1 small bunch (6 to 8 sprigs) Italian flat-leaf parsley

6 ounces (1 ⅓ cups) Parmesan cheese for grating

1 teaspoon ground cinnamon

1 teaspoon nutmeg

1 teaspoon ground allspice

1 teaspoon oregano (preferably Greek)

½ teaspoon salt

¼ teaspoon ground black pepper

1 15 ½ -ounce can chopped tomatoes

1 ½ tablespoons tomato paste mixed with ¼ cup hot water

2 tablespoons butter

¼ cup extra-virgin olive oil (preferably Greek) plus extra if needed

1 pound lean ground lamb or beef

¼ cup plain bread crumbs

BÉCHAMEL SAUCE

2 cups whole milk

2 tablespoons butter

¼ cup all-purpose flour

¼ teaspoon salt

a pinch of grated nutmeg

3 eggs slightly beaten

On your mark . . .

- Wash the eggplant, cut the stem off at the top, and slice off about ¼ inch from the bottom and discard.

- Cut into ⅓-inch-thick slices.

- Lay one slice in the bottom of a large bowl. Sprinkle it with about ¼ teaspoon of salt. Lay another slice in the bowl and sprinkle with salt. Repeat until all the slices are cut, salted, and layered in the bowl.

- Let the eggplant stand for about 30 minutes while you prepare the ground meat filling.

Get set . . .

To prepare the ground meat filling:

- Peel and finely chop the onion, measure 1 ½ cups, and set aside.

- Slightly crush the garlic by laying the flat side of a chef's knife on the clove and pressing evenly to break open the skin. Remove the skin, chop the garlic, and set aside.

- Wash the parsley, shake off the excess water, coarsely chop, measure ¼ cup, and set aside.

- Grate the Parmesan cheese, measure 1 ½ cups, and set aside.

- Combine the cinnamon, nutmeg, allspice, oregano, salt, and pepper in a small bowl and set aside.

- Measure 1 ½ cups of the chopped tomatoes and set aside. Any extra tomatoes can be covered, refrigerated, and used in another recipe.

- Combine the tomato paste with the hot water. Mix well until smooth and set aside.

Cook!

- Heat a 12-to 14-inch skillet over low heat for 30 seconds. You will need a lid for it later.

- Add the butter and 2 tablespoons olive oil to the pan.

- Add the onions and garlic and sauté together for 4 to 5 minutes until translucent. If the garlic begins to brown, turn the heat down.

- Add the ground meat and cook for 4 to 5 minutes or until the meat loses its pink color. Break it up with a wooden spoon as it cooks.

- Skim the fat that rises to the top of the ground meat and discard.
- Add the chopped tomatoes, spice mix, and the tomato paste mixture. Stir well to combine all the ingredients.
- Once the ground meat filling comes to a soft boil, lower the heat to simmer.
- Cover the pan with the lid slightly ajar, and cook for 30 to 40 minutes. This is the ground meat filling.

To prepare the béchamel sauce:

- In a small saucepan, heat the milk over low heat, but don't let it boil.
- In another larger saucepan, melt the butter over low heat. Once it is melted and has stopped bubbling, add the flour. Using a wire whisk or wooden spoon, mix well until combined and thickened. Cook for about 1 minute, stirring constantly to prevent sticking or browning.
- Slowly pour in the warm milk a little at a time. Add the pinch of nutmeg and salt. Stir all the ingredients together into a smooth sauce and cook for about 2 minutes or until slightly thickened.
- Slowly add the slightly beaten eggs and stir well. Return to the burner, lower the heat to simmer, and cook for another minute. Turn off the heat, remove the saucepan from the burner, and let stand. This is the béchamel sauce.
- Set the oven to broil.
- Remove the eggplant slices from the bowl. They will be damp. Brush off the salt and dry each slice with a paper towel.
- Lay the slices on a metal baking sheet.
- Remove 2 tablespoons of the olive oil and set aside.
- Brush each slice (on both sides) with the remaining olive oil.
- Place the eggplant under the broiler for about 4 to 5 minutes on each side.
- Watch the slices closely so they don't burn.
- Turn off the broiler, remove the eggplant, and set aside.
- Grate the cheese, measure 1 cup, and set aside.

- Preheat the oven to 350°F.

- Lightly oil a 9- to 10-inch cast-iron or metal skillet or 10 x 9 x 3-inch baking pan.

- Sprinkle the bread crumbs across the bottom of the pan, tipping it back and forth to evenly cover the bottom and sides.

- Place a layer of the eggplant slices on top of the bread crumbs, covering the bottom of the pan. You may have to cut them to fit.

- Spoon the meat filling on top of the eggplant.

- Spoon the béchamel over the meat filling to cover. Sprinkle on the chopped parsley, then top with the grated cheese.

- Place on the middle rack of the oven and bake for 45 to 50 minutes or until golden brown.

- Let cool 10 to 15 minutes. Slice into squares and serve.

Baked Fish with Bread Crumbs
Psari a la Spetsiota

From the island of Spetses off the eastern coast of the Peloponnese comes this popular and easy-to-prepare recipe. Traditionally this dish calls for four cloves of garlic. You can adjust the amount according to your personal taste. But since garlic is a key flavor in the recipe, why not try it first the authentic way?

Serves 4 to 6

Ingredients

2 pounds red snapper, cod, turbot, scrod, or other boneless fillets about ¾-inch thick

1 lemon

4 fresh ripe plain tomatoes or 1 ½ cups chopped canned tomatoes with their liquid

1 to 4 garlic cloves

4 to 6 sprigs fresh parsley

1 teaspoon salt

freshly ground pepper

½ cup plain, toasted bread crumbs

⅓ cup extra-virgin olive oil (preferably Greek)

On your mark . . .

- Rinse the fish and pat dry. Cut into four equal portions.
- Lay the fish in a 13 x 9-inch ovenproof glass or stainless steel baking pan.
- Squeeze the juice of the lemon through a small hand strainer to catch the seeds.
- Pour the juice over the fish.
- Sprinkle a pinch of salt and pepper on each steak, cover the dish with plastic wrap, and place in the refrigerator.

Get set . . .

- If using fresh tomatoes, wash and cut out the stem circle from the top. Chop the tomatoes into small chunks.

- Measure 1 ½ cups and place in a large bowl. If using canned tomatoes, measure 1 ½ cups, including the liquid, and place in a large bowl.

- Slightly crush the garlic by laying the flat side of a chef's knife on the clove and pressing evenly to break open the skin. Remove the skin, cut the garlic into thin slices, and add to the tomatoes in the bowl.

- Wash the parsley and shake off the excess water.

- Coarsely chop and add to the tomatoes.

- Add the rest of the salt and ¼ teaspoon ground black pepper.

- Mix well and set aside to marinate for 30 minutes, but don't refrigerate it.

- After 15 minutes, preheat the oven to 400°F. Set a timer to help you remember.

Cook!

- Remove the fish from the refrigerator.
- Spoon the tomato mixture evenly over each piece of fish.
- Evenly sprinkle the bread crumbs over the top.
- Drizzle the olive oil over the bread crumbs.
- Place the fish in the preheated oven and bake for 15 minutes.
- After 15 minutes, open the oven and, using a large metal spoon, carefully baste the fish by spooning the liquid in the pan over each piece.
- Bake another 10 minutes and then baste the fish a final time.
- Check to see if the fish is done by gently pressing on it. If it feels firm, it is ready to come out of the oven. If it feels soft, it will need another 5 minutes of baking.
- Serve hot as a main dish, or cold as an appetizer.

Shrimp with Feta Cheese and Tomatoes
Garides Saganaki

The port city of Thessaloniki, the capital of Macedonia, is proud of its cosmopolitan reputation and its local cuisine. Shrimp cooked in a rich sauce of feta and tomatoes is a mainstay of the city's culinary offerings. It is usually served as an appetizer or as a main course in a special baking dish called a *saganaki*. When shopping for this recipe, you'll want to find fresh, large shrimp. Serve it with a simple side dish of boiled rice if you like.

Serves 4

Ingredients

1 ½ pounds large shrimp

1 lemon

1 small white onion

2 garlic cloves

4 to 5 sprigs flat-leaf parsley

4 medium-size ripe tomatoes or 1 28-ounce can chopped tomatoes with liquid

⅓ cup extra-virgin olive oil (preferably Greek)

½ teaspoon dried oregano (preferably Greek)

1 teaspoon sugar

1 ½ cups (8 ounces) crumbled feta cheese

2 cups hot cooked rice (optional)

On your mark, get set . . .

- Peel the shrimp and discard the shells.

- To remove the vein from the shrimp, take each shrimp and lay it flat on its side on a cutting board. Using a paring knife, make a slight cut starting at the top of the curved side, and continue to the tail of the shrimp. You will find a black vein. Pull it out and discard it while rinsing the shrimp under cold running water. Repeat with the rest of the shrimp.

- Place the shrimp in a large bowl. Squeeze the juice from the lemon into a small hand strainer to remove any pits, and pour over the shrimp. Give the shrimp a stir, then refrigerate while you prepare the rest of the ingredients.

- Peel and chop the onion, measure ½ cup, and set aside.
- Slightly crush the garlic by laying the flat side of a chef's knife on the clove and pressing evenly to break open the skin. Remove the skin and chop the garlic and set aside.
- Wash the parsley sprigs and shake off excess water. Coarsely chop and set aside.
- If using fresh tomatoes, wash and remove the stem circle at the top and chop the tomatoes into chunks. Measure 2 cups, making sure to keep as much liquid as possible, and set aside.
- If using canned tomatoes, measure 2 cups and set aside.

Cook!

- In a 10- or 12-inch all-metal or cast-iron frying pan, heat the olive oil over medium-low heat for 30 seconds.
- Add the onion and garlic, and sauté for 4 to 5 minutes. If the garlic begins to brown, turn the heat down.
- Add the tomatoes, parsley, oregano, and sugar. Bring to a boil, reduce the heat to low, and simmer the tomato mixture for 30 minutes. Let it cool for 15 minutes.
- Preheat the oven to 450°F.
- Add the shrimp to the tomato mixture and stir well. If you are not using an ovenproof frying pan, pour the shrimp into a 9 x 12-inch baking dish.
- Sprinkle the crumbled feta over the top and place the dish in the oven.
- Bake for 10 to 12 minutes until the sauce is bubbly, the shrimp are bright pink, and the cheese is melted.
- Serve hot over cooked rice or with some crusty bread.

Baked Macaroni with Cheese and Ground Meat Casserole
Pastitsio

Who doesn't love macaroni and cheese? This recipe takes that famous dish to new heights. *Pastitsio* combines macaroni, cheese, a ground meat filling, and a creamy topping of béchamel sauce. This is real Greek comfort food. The recipe involves several steps, but sometimes the really great dishes take a little longer to prepare. The compliments you will receive from everyone at the table will more than make up for the extra time spent in the kitchen.

Serves 6 to 8

Ingredients

GROUND MEAT FILLING

2 small white onions

1 garlic clove

1 small bunch (6 to 8 sprigs) Italian flat-leaf parsley

6 ounces (1 ½ cups) of Parmesan cheese for grating

1 teaspoon ground cinnamon

¼ teaspoon ground nutmeg

1 teaspoon ground allspice

1 teaspoon dried oregano (preferably Greek)

½ teaspoon salt

¼ teaspoon ground black pepper

1 15 ½-ounce can chopped tomatoes

1 ½ tablespoons tomato paste mixed with
    ¼ cup hot water

2 tablespoons butter

2 tablespoons extra-virgin olive oil (preferably Greek)

1 pound lean ground lamb or beef

1 pound elbow macaroni

½ teaspoon salt

3 tablespoons of extra-virgin olive oil

¼ cup plain bread crumbs

BÉCHAMEL SAUCE

2 cups whole milk

2 tablespoons butter

¼ cup all-purpose flour

½ teaspoon salt

a pinch of grated nutmeg

3 eggs slightly beaten

On your mark . . .

To prepare the ground meat filling:

- Peel and finely chop the onions, measure 1 ½ cups, and set aside.

- Slightly crush the garlic by laying the flat side of a chef's knife on the clove and pressing evenly to break open the skin. Remove the skin and chop the garlic and set aside.

- Wash the parsley, shake off the excess water, coarsely chop, measure ¼ cup, and set aside.

Get set . . .

- Grate the Parmesan cheese, measure 1 ½ cups, and set aside.

- Combine the cinnamon, nutmeg, allspice, oregano, salt, and pepper in a small bowl and set aside.

- Measure 1 ½ cups of the chopped tomatoes and set aside. Any extra tomatoes can be covered, refrigerated and used in another recipe.

- Combine the tomato paste with the hot water. Mix well until smooth and set aside.

Cook!

- Heat a 12- to 14-inch skillet over low heat for 30 seconds. You will need a lid for it later.

- Add the butter and 2 tablespoons olive oil to the pan.

- Add the onions and garlic and sauté together for 4 to 5 minutes until translucent. If the garlic begins to brown, turn the heat down.

- Add the ground meat and cook for 4 to 5 minutes or until the meat loses its pink color. Break it up with a wooden spoon as it cooks.

- Skim the fat that rises to the top of the ground meat and discard.

- Add the chopped tomatoes, spice mix, and the tomato paste mixture. Stir well to combine all the ingredients.

- Once the ground meat filling comes to a soft boil, lower the heat to simmer.

- Cover the pan with the lid slightly ajar, and cook for 30 to 40 minutes. That is the ground meat filling.
- Bring 5 to 6 quarts of water to a boil.
- Add the macaroni and salt, and cook for 6 to 8 minutes. The macaroni should be just underdone or slightly hard in the center.
- Drain the macaroni in a colander but don't rinse.
- Pour the drained macaroni back into the pot it was just cooked in and add ½ cup of the grated cheese and 2 tablespoons of olive oil. Stir well then set aside.

To prepare the béchamel sauce:

- In a small saucepan, heat the milk over low heat, but don't let it boil.
- In another larger saucepan, melt the butter over low heat. Once it is melted and has stopped bubbling, add the flour. Using a wire whisk or wooden spoon, mix well until combined.
- Cook for about 1 minute, stirring constantly to prevent sticking or browning.
- Slowly pour in about ½ cup of the warm milk. Stir well to combine with the flour and butter.
- Add the next ½ cup and stir until combined.
- Repeat with the rest of the milk, in ½ cup additions, until all the milk is added and the mixture is smooth.
- Add the pinch of nutmeg and salt.
- Cook for about 3 minutes or until slightly thickened, stirring constantly.
- Remove the pan from the heat and slowly add the slightly beaten eggs. Stir well.
- Return to the burner, lower the heat to simmer, and cook for another 2 minutes, stirring to prevent sticking.
- Turn off the heat, remove the pan from the burner and let stand. This is the béchamel sauce.
- Preheat the oven to 350°F.
- Lightly coat the bottom and sides of a 9 x 12 x 2½-inch deep

baking pan or cast-iron skillet with the remaining tablespoon of olive oil.

- Sprinkle the bread crumbs over the bottom of the baking pan.
- Evenly cover the pan with ½ of the cooked macaroni.
- Spread on the ground meat filling to evenly cover the macaroni.
- Sprinkle half of the remaining grated cheese over the meat filling.
- Add the rest of the macaroni over the filling.
- Spoon the béchamel sauce over the macaroni.
- To finish, sprinkle the remaining grated cheese evenly over the top.
- Place the baking pan on the middle rack of the oven and bake for 40 to 50 minutes, or until the top is golden brown.
- Let cool for 10 minutes, cut into squares, and then serve.

Roast Leg of Lamb
Arni sto Fourno

What's the real star of Greek cuisine? If you asked Greek cooks, the answer might be roast leg of lamb. The Greeks are masters at cooking lamb in stews and savory appetizers or roasting it in the oven or over open fires to bring out its natural flavor. This recipe, from the island of Naxos in the Aegean Sea, is ideal for a holiday meal or any special occasion. When shopping for this recipe, look for a lean cut of lamb.

Serves 6 to 8

Ingredients

1 large garlic clove

1 bunch green onions

1 small yellow onion

2 lemons

4 to 6 Idaho or russet potatoes

5- to 6-pound leg of lamb

2 teaspoons salt

½ teaspoon freshly ground black pepper

2 teaspoons dried oregano (preferably Greek)

⅓ cup extra-virgin olive oil (preferably Greek)

1 to 2 cups boiling water

On your mark . . .

- Slightly crush the garlic by laying the flat side of a chef's knife on the clove and pressing firmly to break open the skin. Remove the skin and set the clove aside.

- Wash the green onions, remove any dark or damaged outer leaves, and cut off the root end.

- Cut the green onions, including a few inches of the green tops, into 1 ½-inch slices. Measure 1 cup and set aside.

- Peel and cut the onion in half, then cut each half into thin slices. Measure 1 cup and set aside.

- Cut the lemons in half. Use a fruit juicer to extract the juice and pour the juice through a hand strainer over a small bowl to remove any seeds.

- Measure ⅓ cup of juice and set aside.
- Wash and slice the potatoes crosswise into ½-inch slices. Place the potatoes in a bowl and cover with cold water and set aside.

Get set . . .

- Preheat the oven to 450°F.
- Cut away any excess fat from the outside of the leg of lamb.
- Cut the garlic clove into 6 to 8 thin slices.
- Using the tip of a sharp knife make several small slits about ½-inch deep, spaced evenly apart, in the surface of the meat including the top and sides.

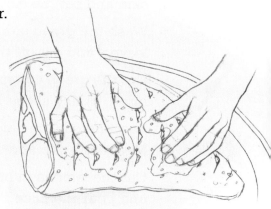

- Place a slice of the garlic into each of the slits. This will help flavor the roast.
- Place a metal rack inside a roasting pan just large enough to hold the lamb and sliced potatoes.
- Lay the lamb on the rack, fat side up.
- Add the salt, pepper, dried oregano, and olive oil to the lemon juice and stir to combine.
- Remove 3 tablespoons of the mixture and set aside.
- Pour the rest over the lamb and, with your very clean hands, rub the mixture evenly into the leg of lamb.
- Wash your hands with hot soapy water.

Cook!

- Drain the potatoes in a colander.
- Spread a few sheets of paper towel on the countertop and lay the drained potatoes on the paper towels. Dry the slices and place in a large bowl.
- Add the chopped green and yellow onions to the potatoes, along with the reserved 3 tablespoons of lemon and

olive oil mixture and toss well to coat the potatoes and onions.

- Evenly distribute the potatoes and onions around the lamb in the bottom of the roasting pan.

- Place the pan on the middle rack of the oven and immediately lower the temperature to 375°F.

- After 30 minutes, carefully add the boiling water to the bottom of the pan.

- Continue to roast the lamb for 2 ½ hours, basting every 45 minutes or so with the pan juices.

- Don't let the liquid dry out in the pan as the lamb is baking. You may need to add ½ to ¾ cup additional water.

- When cooked, the lamb should be tender. Use a meat thermometer to get it just right. It should read 155°F for rare, 160°F for medium, and 165 to 170°F for well done.

- Remove the roast from the oven and check the potatoes. If they need more cooking time, lift the roast out of the pan and place it on an additional roasting pan or baking tray. Cover it loosely with aluminum foil and let it rest for 10 to 15 minutes before carving. This allows the juices, which have come to the surface during roasting, to flow back to the center of the meat.

- Return the potatoes to the oven to finish cooking.

- Slice the roast and serve hot with the potatoes and any pan drippings.

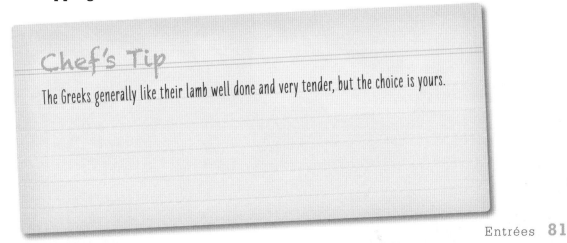

Chef's Tip

The Greeks generally like their lamb well done and very tender, but the choice is yours.

Desserts

Yogurt and Honey with Strawberries
Yaourti me Fraoula kai Meli

The yogurt in Greece is so good it might be mistaken for whipping cream. Blended with fresh strawberries and honey, it makes for a simple but unforgettable dessert. The Greeks make yogurt from whole sheep's milk as well as cow's milk, so it's richer and creamier than what we're used to. You might find Greek-style yogurt in a local specialty market. Today yogurt made from sheep's milk is growing in popularity and can be found in many health-food stores and supermarkets. But if you can't find it, follow the recipe on page 25 to create your own.

Serves 6

Ingredients

2 cups fresh strawberries

2 tablespoons sugar

2 cups plain yogurt or Greek-style yogurt (page 25)

½ cup honey (preferably Greek)

¼ cup slivered almonds, or chopped walnuts or pistachios (optional)

On your mark, get set . . .

- Wash the strawberries and let them drain in a colander, tossing lightly, to remove any excess water.

- Cut away any dark spots or soft brown sections from the berries.

- Remove the stems. The tip of a teaspoon works well for this.

- Slice the strawberries in quarters and place in a large bowl.

- Sprinkle with the sugar and refrigerate for 15 to 20 minutes.

- Combine the yogurt and honey in another bowl and mix until they have just started to combine. Be careful not to overmix.

- Chill for 15 to 20 minutes.

Serve!

- Remove the fruit and yogurt.

- Stir the fruit to combine the strawberries and the juice together.

- You will need six individual serving dishes or tall dessert glasses.

- Spoon enough fruit to fill about one-quarter of the dessert dish.

- Add a tablespoon of the yogurt mixture on top. Spoon on more fruit followed by the yogurt mixture.

- Top with the slivered nuts and serve cold.

Chef's Tip

You can substitute raspberries, peaches, blackberries, or any fresh fruit in season for this recipe.

Yogurt Cake with Fresh Orange Syrup
Ravani

The Greek art of pastry making is centuries old. The region of Macedonia gives us this traditional syrup-soaked yogurt cake. *Ravani* combines a delicate golden sponge cake made with farina and a fruit-flavored syrup to create a memorable dessert.

Serves 8 to 10

Ingredients

SYRUP

4 to 6 oranges

2 lemons

1 ¼ cups confectioners' sugar

CAKE

2 cups all-purpose flour

1 cup Cream of Wheat (not instant) or farina

1 ½ teaspoons baking powder

¼ teaspoon baking soda

1 ½ sticks unsalted butter

1 cup granulated sugar

5 large eggs

1 cup Greek-style yogurt (page 25) or sour cream

¼ cup confectioners' sugar for dusting

On your mark, get set . . .

- Wash the oranges and lemons.

- Using a potato peeler or sharp knife, remove six 1-inch-wide by 3-inch-long strips from the orange peel and set aside. Be careful not to cut too deeply and remove any white part from the skin as it will add a bitter flavor.

- Cut the oranges in half.

- Use a fruit juicer to squeeze the oranges. Strain the juice through a small hand strainer to catch any seeds.

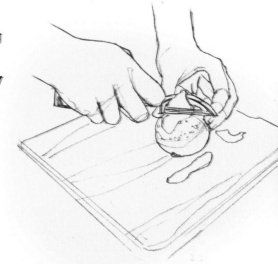

- Measure 1 ½ cups juice and pour into a medium-size bowl.

- Repeat this step with the lemons, measuring ½ cup, and combine with the orange juice. Add three of the peeled orange strips to the juice and set aside.

- Lay the other three orange strips on top of each other and cut them into long thin strips. Then cut, or mince the strips into tiny pieces and put in a small bowl and set aside.

Cook!

- Put the confectioners' sugar, orange peel, and the citrus juices in a 2- to 3-quart saucepan and place over low heat.

- Stir well to dissolve the sugar and combine all the ingredients.

- Heat the mixture slowly and bring to a gentle boil. This will take 6 to 8 minutes. Reduce to a simmer and let it cook, uncovered, for 20 minutes while you prepare the cake. This is the syrup.

- Preheat the oven to 350°F.

- Butter a 12 x 18-inch ovenproof baking pan and set aside.

- Combine the flour, Cream of Wheat or farina, baking powder, and baking soda together in a medium bowl. Sift the combined ingredients into a separate bowl.

- Melt the butter slowly over low heat, being careful it doesn't burn.

- In a large bowl, beat the eggs on high with an electric mixer for 2 minutes, or until light and foamy.

- Add the granulated sugar and the minced orange pieces and continue to beat for another 1 to 2 minutes, or until the eggs and sugar are smooth, golden, and creamy.

- Turn the beater to low and add about 1 cup of the flour mixture and blend well.

- Add a little of the melted butter and blend well.

- Add another cup of the flour mixture and then a little more of the butter.

- Continue until all the butter and flour are combined into a smooth batter.

- Turn off the mixer and remove the beaters. Using a rubber spatula, scrape off any batter from the beaters into the bowl.

- Add the yogurt or sour cream to the bowl. With a rubber spatula or wooden spoon, fold, or gently combine, the ingredients in the batter.

- Pour the batter into the buttered baking pan.

- Place the pan on the middle rack of the oven and bake the cake for 45 minutes to 1 hour until golden brown and firm when pressed lightly in its center.

- Remove the cake from the oven and place on a wire rack.

- Make several holes in the surface of the cake with a butter knife or a wooden chopstick.

- Remove the strips of orange peels from the syrup and discard. Now pour the syrup evenly over the top of the cake.

- Let the cake stand at least 2 hours to absorb the syrup.

- When you are ready to serve the cake, place the confectioners' sugar in a hand strainer and gently tap the side to sprinkle the sugar over the top. Cut into small squares and serve.

BAKING PAN

ELECTRIC JUICER

MIXING BOWLS, ASSORTED

LARGE METAL SPOON

CHEESECLOTH

FOUR-SIDED GRATER

HAND JUICER

SPATULA

COLANDER

KNIVES, ASSORTED

VEGETABLE PEELER

STOCKPOT

COOKIE SHEETS

LADLE

SALAD SPINNER

STRAINER

CUTTING BOARD

MEASURING CUPS

SAUCEPANS WITH LIDS,
ASSORTED SIZES

TONGS

ELECTRIC HAND MIXER

MEASURING SPOONS

SKILLETS

WHISK

Allspice

These dried berries from Jamaica are available whole or ground. If you have a spice grinder, it is best to buy them whole and grind them yourself for maximum flavor.

Bay Leaf

This herb is very popular in Mediterranean cooking. The hot, sunny climate of Greece is ideal for growing and drying bay leaves. They have a distinctive flavor and should be used in small amounts. You should always remove the bay leaf from the dish you have prepared just before serving it.

Bread Crumbs

The best bread crumbs are the ones you make yourself. Stale or hardened bread is ideal. Grate it with a hand grater, using the tiniest holes. (Be careful not to grate your knuckles along with the bread!) If you don't want to make them yourself, you can easily buy bread crumbs. Look for the ones marked "plain." They will have no salt or extra seasoning. That way you can season them yourself.

Cloves

A clove is the tiny dried flower bud of an evergreen tree. It is popular in Greek cooking for its rich flavor. It comes whole or ground. If you buy it whole and grind it yourself, you're assured the best flavor. It should be used carefully because the flavor of cloves can overpower the other flavors in your recipe.

Dill

Dill is a member of the parsley family. It comes both fresh and dried. Because of the mild climate in Greece, cooks there grow it almost year round. When shopping for fresh dill, let your nose be your guide. Look for bright green bunches without dark spots and a definite "pickle" smell. Dill will need to be kept refrigerated and washed thoroughly before using it.

Eggplant

The eggplant is one food that is a little confused. It's really a fruit, not a vegetable. It gets its name from its egg-like shape. The eggplants most familiar to us in North America are the large purple ones. But eggplants can be white or light purple, round or long and thin like an oversized carrot. When shopping for eggplants look for firm, solid ones without brown spots or shriveled skin. Keep them refrigerated until ready to use.

Farina

Farina is hard wheat flour. That means it is harvested late in the season when the wheat has reached full maturity and then ground into flour. Look for Cream of Wheat, a combination of farina and wheat, for the recipes in this book.

Garlic

Garlic is a member of the onion family, and it adds valuable flavor in Greek cooking. When you purchase garlic, look for large bulbs that are hard and solid. Inside the bulb are cloves. To work with the cloves, first separate them from the bulb. With the flat side of a knife, give them a good whack, then remove the white, paperlike skin and cut off the dark tip. The cloves can be chopped into small pieces, mashed, or cut into thin slices. Many nutritionists believe that garlic has great health benefits because it is rich in minerals. The world is separated into two groups of people—those who love garlic and those who don't. Which are you?

Lentils

The lentil has been around for such a long time that it has been found in prehistoric sites in Europe. It comes in a variety of colors—red, yellow, gray, and even pink. Lentils are packed with protein and flavor. Before you use dried lentils, it is essential that you rinse them and carefully check to remove anything that is not a lentil, such as small stones. Dried lentils can be kept in an airtight container for a long time.

Nutmeg

This spice is native to Indonesia but popular in Greece. But be careful! Nutmeg can dominate the flavor of a dish, so don't overdo it. It is best to buy it whole and grate only what you need for your recipe. Store the nutmeg sealed in a glass jar, and it will keep a long time.

Olive Oil

Read more about olive oil on page 22.

Oregano

Dried or fresh, this pungent herb is full of flavor. It is perfect for salad dressings, soups, tomato, chicken, and vegetable dishes. Used correctly, it is an essential part of the flavor of Greek cooking. Dried oregano, stored in a covered glass jar, will keep for about six months.

Parsley, Italian Flat-Leaf

This variety of parsley, sometimes called Italian parsley, is full of flavor. Look for bright green leaves and avoid bunches that are wilted or shriveled. Be sure you don't make a common mistake and buy coriander, a similar-looking herb, which is sometimes called Chinese parsley. Wash the parsley before you use it. When you chop it, remove the stems and discard. Use just the leaves to get the best flavor.

Pepper, Whole Black

There is a real difference in the flavor of black pepper when it is freshly ground from a pepper mill. You are probably most familiar with the ground pepper that you buy in the store. Chances are it was ground months earlier and the flavor has weakened. Use black pepper with caution as it can make your dish very hot.

Thyme

This herb is used in all regions of Greece. The leaves can be used fresh or dried. Check the recipe to see which is recommended.

Tomatoes

There is no doubt that the tomato is a key ingredient in many Greek dishes. When shopping for fresh tomatoes look for a nice rich, red color and avoid ones with spots or bruises. If you are unable to find good fresh tomatoes, don't hesitate to buy canned. To store fresh tomatoes, keep them away from heat, but never put them in the refrigerator. The cold will destroy their flavor and texture.

Yogurt

Yogurt is the health food that tastes like it's not—rich and creamy, but good for us, too. Greek yogurt, made generally from sheep's milk, is flavorful, and is similar to heavy cream. Yogurt can also be made from the milk of cows, goats, or even buffalo. If you can't find Greek-style yogurt in your neighborhood, follow the recipe on page 25 to make your own. Always purchase yogurt as far as possible from the expiration date on the container and keep it refrigerated.

Find Out More/Metric Conversion Chart

Books

Gifford, Clive. *Food and Cooking in Ancient Greece*. New York: Powerkids Press, 2010.

Orr, Tamra B. *The Food of Greece* (Flavors of the World). Tarrytown, NY: Marshall Cavendish Benchmark Books, 2012.

Sheen, Barbara. *Foods of Greece*. Farmington Hills, MI: Kidhaven Press, 2006.

Websites
Ancient Greece

http://greece.mrdonn.org/
Learn all about ancient Greek culture, from maps and geography to daily life and sports.

Greek Culture

www.greeka.com
Information about the culture of Greece.

Metric Conversion Chart You can use the chart below to convert from U.S. measurements to the metric system.

Weight
1 ounce = 28 grams
½ pound (8 ounces) = 227 grams
1 pound = .45 kilogram
2.2 pounds = 1 kilogram

Liquid volume
1 teaspoon = 5 milliliters
1 tablespoon = 15 milliliters
1 fluid ounce = 30 milliliters
1 cup = 240 milliliters (.24 liter)
1 pint = 480 milliliters (.48 liter)
1 quart = .95 liter

Length
¼ inch = .6 centimeter
½ inch = 1.25 centimeters
1 inch = 2.5 centimeters

Temperature
100°F = 40°C
110°F = 45°C
212°F = 100°C (boiling point of water)
350°F = 180°C
375°F = 190°C
400°F = 200°C
425°F = 220°C
450°F = 235°C

(To convert temperatures in Fahrenheit to Celsius, subtract 32 and multiply by .56)

Index

Page numbers in **boldface** are photographs.

Chef Matthew Locricchio knows a thing or two about cooking. What sets this chef apart from other talented professionals in his field is his knack for imparting this culinary wisdom to children. Matthew was born in Michigan and into a restaurant and catering family, and has spent most of his life in the food industry. Along with his years of training as a chef and his numerous books on cooking, Matthew has made guest appearances on Martha Stewart Radio, *Everyday Food* to talk about his unique approach to getting kids interested in cooking. He has also been heard on *The Faith Middleton Show: Food Schmooze*, on National Public Radio (NPR), and seen on WGN TV, *Lunch Break*, in Chicago.

Matthew's award-winning *The 2nd International Cookbook for Kids* followed up on his earlier *The International Cookbook for Kids*, and, much like the first book, is full of delicious, kid-friendly recipes from around the world.

Also a playwright and actor, Matthew has worked in numerous commercials, soap operas, films, and television shows. Chef Locricchio has been a guest instructor at The Institute of Culinary Education in New York City and Stonewall Kitchen in York, Maine. He guest lectures in the series "Adventures in the Global Kitchen for Kids and Families" at The American Museum of Natural History in New York City.

His brand new *Teen Cuisine*, with spectacular photos by James Beard Winner, James Peterson, was released October 1, 2010. He is currently writing a follow-up with a vegetarian cookbook.

More information about Matthew Locricchio can be found at his website: www.cookbooksandkids.com or www.teencuisinebooks.com